Colonial Keyboard Tunes

SET FOR PIANO OR HARPSICHORD

by

J. S. DARLING

Organist and Choirmaster of
Bruton Parish Church in Williamsburg
Harpsichordist and Musical
Consultant to Colonial Williamsburg

The Colonial Williamsburg Foundation
Williamsburg, Virginia

Library of Congress Cataloging in Publication Data
Colonial Keyboard Tunes
1. Piano music, Arranged.   2. Harpsichord music, Arranged.
3. Dance music, American.
I. Darling, James S.
M32.8.C655   786.4'052   80-12691
ISBN 0-87935-055-5

Printed in the United States of America

Colonial Keyboard Tunes

CONTENTS

v

PREFACE

"THE GENTM. AND LADIES here are perfectly well bred, not an ill Dancer in my Govmt." So wrote Governor William Gooch on December 28, 1727, soon after he arrived in Williamsburg. Any occasion was an excuse for a ball, and the annual celebration of the King's "Birth-Night" became an important social event at the Governor's Palace. A lavish dinner preceded an evening of dancing, and once Governor Gooch had to disburse one hundred guineas from his private purse to cover the cost and especially to resupply the wine cellar.

In 1751, during the administration of Robert Dinwiddie, an elegant ballroom and supper room were added to the Palace, with the wing projecting into the garden. Similar reception halls were built at plantation houses where hospitable families entertained their guests. Traveling dancing masters like Francis Christian journeyed from place to place teaching the latest steps. At Nomini Hall, home of wealthy Robert Carter, Mr. Christian was described as "punctual, and rigid in his discipline, so strict indeed that he struck two of the young Misses for a fault in the course of their performance, even in the presence of the Mother of one of them." Nevertheless, he was repeatedly invited back, his return eagerly anticipated.

Usually black musicians, especially fiddlers, provided dance music. Negroes who played the violin were advertised for sale in the *Virginia Gazette*, and one exceptional slave performed well on French horn, flute, and other instruments. Sy Gilliat, body servant to Lord Botetourt, became the semiofficial fiddler at state functions in Williamsburg. He is reputed to have dressed in grand style, choosing from a wardrobe of fifty suits passed down by his masters. After the Revolution he was still active in Richmond, the new capital of Virginia, performing with an assistant, "London Briggs," who played the flute and clarinet.

The Bolling manuscript, from which the tunes in this book are drawn, is a rare surviving collection of popular music from the colonial period. The opening "Tally Ho" with its descriptive horn fanfares recalls famous Virginia fox hunters like George Washington. "Monsieur Vallouis Minuet" may have arrived with French troops at the battle of Yorktown. The engaging "Regatta Minuet" might well have been played following tidewater boat races because the diarist Philip Fithian noted, "Both the Rowers and dancers . . . will perspire freely — Or in plain English they will soak in Sweat!" The "Peasants' Dance from Queen Mab" occurs in a popular theatrical afterpiece by the comic actor Henry Woodward. "Miss Ford Dances" has been set in a style appropriate to puppets or marionettes. The "Minuet of Mr. Howard" shows admirable melodic flow, while his "Musette" demonstrates the uneven rhythm of the Scotch snap. "Rural Felicity" anticipates the sentimental parlor ballad. "The Marquis of Granby's March" could have accompanied the opening procession of a colonial ball. An infectious "Jig," untitled in the manuscript, illustrates a contemporary description: "Toward the close of an evening, when the company are pretty well tired of country dances, it is usual to dance jigs, a practice originally borrowed from the negroes." The steps are of "an irregular fantastical nature" with both ladies and gentlemen cutting in at will.

Again we acknowledge the kind permission of the Southern Historical Collection at the University of North Carolina Library in making these tunes available. For a brief account of the Bolling manuscript, see *A Little Keyboard Book*, J. S. Darling, ed. (Williamsburg, Va., 1972). The arrangements are the responsibility of the editor, and the use of a violin to double the melody is authentic practice. Dr. John Molnar, Farmville, Virginia, assisted in historical research, and Mr. Jeffrey Dean, Chicago, Illinois, prepared the final copy of the music. Many of these pieces are recorded on "Peter Pelham's Music," which features sacred and secular music played by the eighteenth-century organist, Peter Pelham. It is available from the Colonial Williamsburg Foundation.

TALLY HO

3

MONSIEUR VALLOUIS MINUET

THE REGATTA MINUET

THE PEASANTS' DANCE FROM QUEEN MAB

MISS FORD DANCES

10

A MINUET BY MR. HOWARD

14

15

A MUSETTE BY MR. HOWARD

RURAL FELICITY — A SONG

THE MARQUIS OF GRANBY'S MARCH

A JIG

23